SIDE B

1. Phantom Lord
2. No Remorse
3. Seek & Destroy
4. Metal Militia

For my son, Neken.

METALLICA

The Unauthorized Biography

Words by Soledad Romero Mariño
Illustrated by David Navas

sourcebooks
eXplore

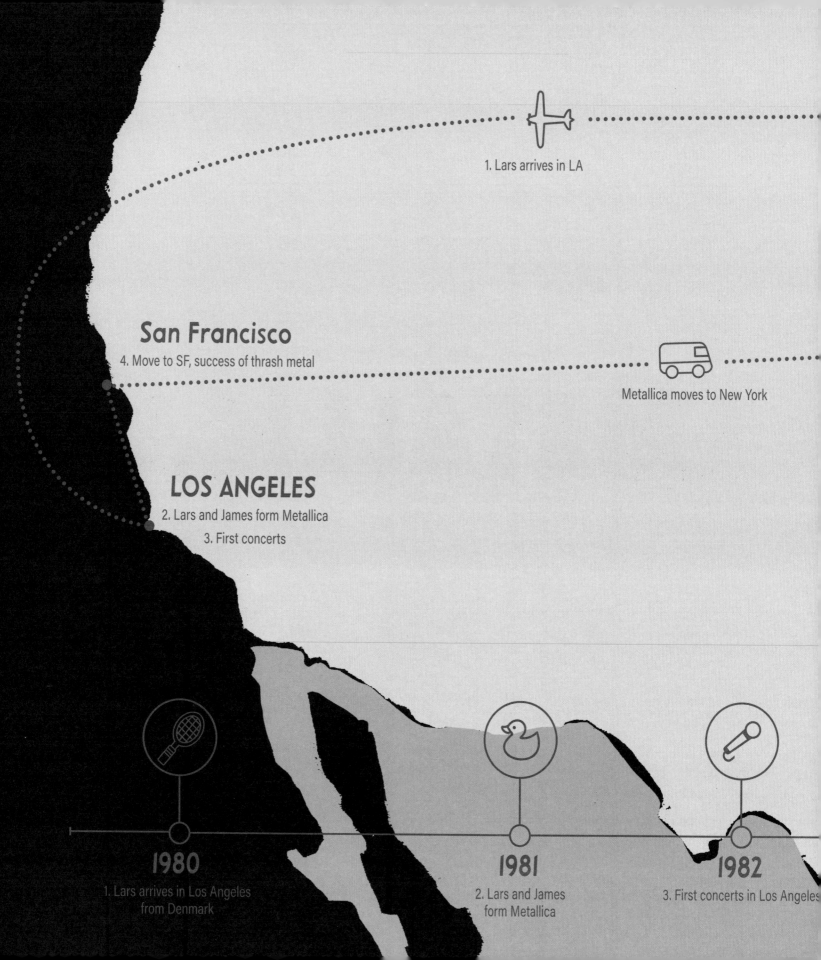

1. Lars arrives in LA

Metallica moves to New York

San Francisco
4. Move to SF, success of thrash metal

LOS ANGELES
2. Lars and James form Metallica
3. First concerts

1980
1. Lars arrives in Los Angeles
from Denmark

1981
2. Lars and James
form Metallica

1982
3. First concerts in Los Angeles

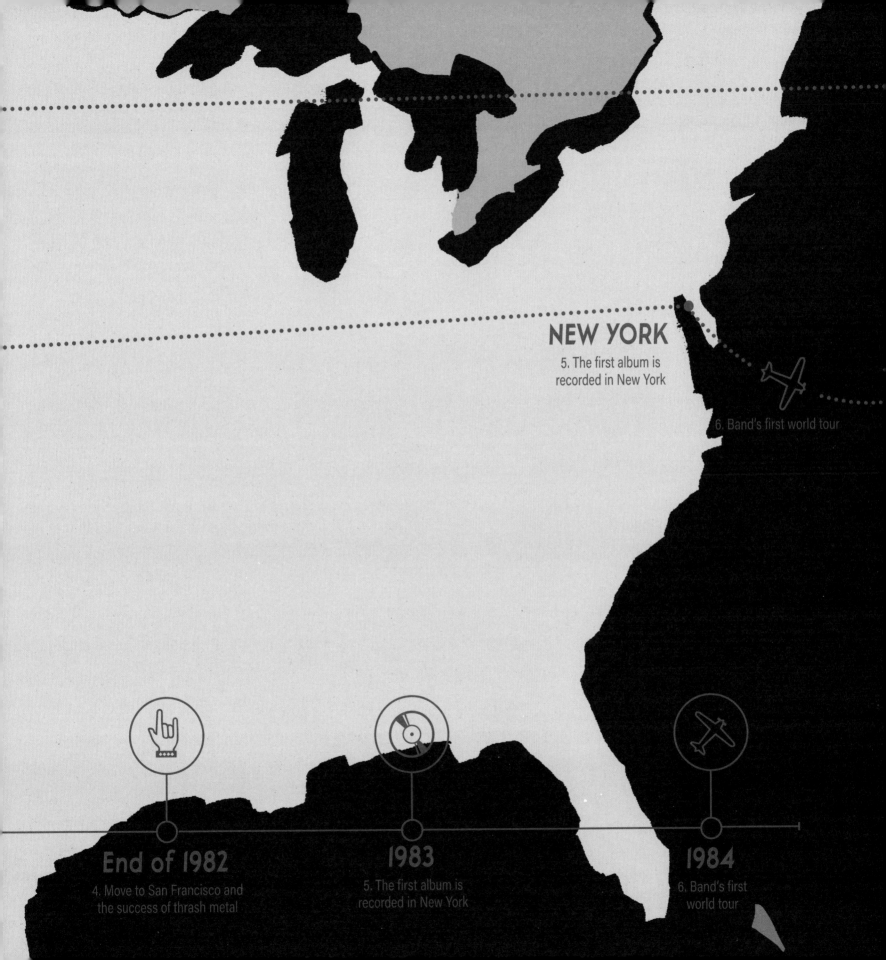

NEW YORK

5. The first album is recorded in New York

6. Band's first world tour

End of 1982

4. Move to San Francisco and the success of thrash metal

1983

5. The first album is recorded in New York

1984

6. Band's first world tour

LARS ULRICH ARRIVES IN LOS ANGELES

In 1980, seventeen-year-old Lars Ulrich from Denmark arrived in Los Angeles with his father and an ambition to become a tennis player. There were many long days of training under the sun, and though Lars was skilled with the racket, his real passion was off the courts.

He was a young fan of classic heavy metal. After tennis practice, Lars spent hours playing the drums and going through record stores in search of new bands to listen to.

Lars discovered the incredible world of metal in the California underground, where young people made music their religion.

A HEAVY METAL BAND

Little by little, Lars became a true metalhead. The young drummer let his hair grow long, started wearing T-shirts with images of metal bands, and rehearsed nonstop.

His passion was unstoppable, and he realized he was better at music than he was at playing tennis. That was the inspiration he needed to leave tennis behind and form his own band.

About a year after moving to the United States, the daring teenager put an ad in a newspaper seeking musicians to join him in this new adventure.

JAMES HETFIELD AND LARS ULRICH FORM METALLICA

From the outskirts of Los Angeles, James Hetfield, a great guitarist and composer, answered Lars's ad. Their meeting was pure dynamite. Lars and James were two kids crazy about metal with hopes to conquer the world.

That's when they created the band they called Metallica. James was the voice, the guitar, and the one who took the creative reins. Lars stuck with the drums.

FIRST STEPS

Lars and James moved into a house that was going to be torn down and set up a place to rehearse. There they started working together with other friends in the new band. They had a great time sharing their passion for heavy metal.

However, they were just a few disheveled teenagers with acne and little experience, and the metal sound demanded power and a heart-attack rhythm. They weren't ready yet.

DAVE MUSTAINE, THE GUITARIST

Metallica definitely needed reinforcements.

One day, the devastatingly talented guitar player Dave Mustaine showed up at rehearsal. Five minutes were enough to destroy the young men with his guitar. His melodies were magic and his devilish riffs thundered in the room.

With him, the band finally had the fury and electricity it needed. Dave became the lead guitar player of Metallica.

GLAM VS. THRASH

Metallica was gaining fans, but it was difficult to find places to perform. On the stages in Los Angeles, the most popular style of music was glam metal, a softer style of metal made to please the masses.

Compared with the glam metal bands, the young men of Metallica were considered noisy and rude. Metallica felt that glam was a betrayal of "real" metal. Their style was a much harder, punk-inspired version of metal. Many called Metallica's music speed metal, power metal, and ultimately, thrash metal.

THE BASSIST CLIFF BURTON

One night at a concert in Los Angeles, Lars and James discovered an extraordinary bass player.

He lit up the stage, shredding on his bass. His fingers flew, invisible, firing notes at extreme speed. His name was Cliff Burton, and he was the missing piece they needed.

Cliff saw clearly that Los Angeles did not understand Metallica's music. So when they asked him to join the band, he had only one condition: they needed to move to San Francisco.

WELCOME TO SAN FRANCISCO

The band members loaded their things into a truck and started for San Francisco. Finally a complete band, Lars, James, Dave, and Cliff were invincible. Thirsty for success, they found a fan base that resonated with their music.

The concerts were a real outpouring of power. The band and spectators flipped their long hair to the frenetic rhythm of the music, sang their songs loudly, and wore torn shirts, jeans, and vests with patches.

They showed off a wild look and claimed pure heavy metal as theirs.

FIRST DEMOS

In San Francisco, Metallica recorded their best songs on tape and sent about twenty copies to people they knew in the music industry.

One of the tapes fell into the hands of Johnny Zazula, a music rep from New York. When he hit play, the music blew his mind. He could immediately hear the band's talent.

Zazula called the group to see if he could represent them and get them their first record deal; Metallica had in their hands the opportunity they were looking for.

They crossed the country from San Francisco to New York, where they lived days and nights of nonstop music.

KIRK HAMMETT, THE NEW GUITARIST

New York was a party. Lars, James, Dave, and Cliff felt like they were on the crest of the wave, but one day something broke.

Repeated arguments between Dave and the band led to his expulsion from Metallica. The great guitarist packed up his things and headed to the bus station. Dave returned to Los Angeles crushed, but with the firm promise to continue playing the strongest and fastest thrash metal on the planet.

After that hard blow for the band and its followers came Kirk Hammett. This young man had the rare guitar skills to replace Dave. Kirk was the person that Metallica needed, and he brought a new sound.

RECORDING THE FIRST ALBUM

While refining this new group, Johnny Zazula met with New York record labels, all unsuccessfully. No one was betting on the first Metallica album.

It was then that Zazula and his wife, sure of the talent of the band, created their own record label, Megaforce Records.

At last, the band entered the recording studio.

They were pure electricity, speed, and strength, and nothing else sounded quite like they did. The album, Kill 'Em All, was an explosive hit and, a few weeks later, the world was beginning to talk about Metallica.

WORLD TOUR

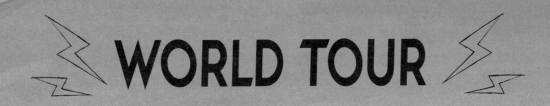

The bandmates went on tour to promote their first album. It was an amazing trip around the world.

James, Lars, Cliff, and Kirk arrived in each city as true rock stars. They were sensational live, and the audience was crazy for the strength and sounds of their concerts.

Metallica was the band of the moment. It was as strong as steel and burned like fire. The band became the symbol of the new thrash metal and traveled the roads, leaving behind miles and miles of music.

METALLICA
IS THE...
WORLD
TO ME

IT ALWAYS HAS BEEN,
AND THAT'S
NOT GOING
TO CHANGE.
I'M MARRIED TO METALLICA.

—JAMES HETFIELD

METALLICA STUDIO ALBUMS

⚡ KILL 'EM ALL (1983)

⚡ RIDE THE LIGHTNING (1984)

⚡ MASTER OF PUPPETS (1986)

⚡ ...AND JUSTICE FOR ALL (1988)

⚡ METALLICA (THE BLACK ALBUM) (1991)

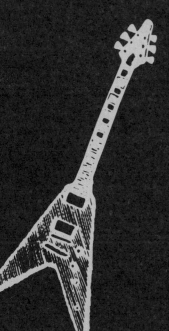

LOAD (1996)

RELOAD (1997)

ST. ANGER (2003)

DEATH MAGNETIC (2008)

HARDWIRED...TO SELF-DESTRUCT (2016)

Metallica has gone on to release albums for decades. They have been inducted into the Rock and Roll Hall of Fame. Their passion for metal and creating music has inspired and will continue to inspire musicians forever.

LEARN MORE ABOUT THE HISTORY OF MUSIC WITH THESE GREAT BOOKS.

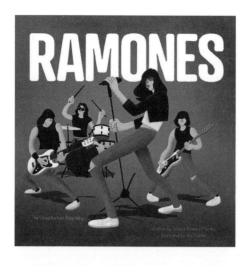

The incredible story of four friends who became legends of punk rock.

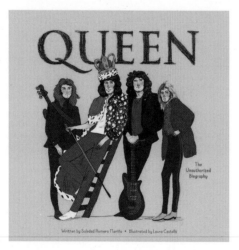

The origin of one of the most ambitious and theatrical rock bands.

The origin of the band that conquered the world with electronic music.

First published in the United States in 2020 by Sourcebooks

Text © 2017, 2020 by Soledad Romero Mariño
Illustrations © 2017, 2020 by David Navas
Cover and internal design © 2020 by Sourcebooks
Cover design by Brittany Vibbert/Sourcebooks
Internal Images © by Freepik, IgorKrapar/Shuttertstock, thedafkish/GettyImages, albertc111/GettyImages

Published by Sourcebooks eXplore, an imprint of Sourcebooks Kids
P.O. Box 4410, Naperville, Illinois 60567–4410
(630) 961-3900
sourcebookskids.com

Originally published as Band Records: *Metallica* in 2017 by Reservoir Kids, an imprint of Penguin Random House Grupo Editorial.

Library of Congress Cataloging-in-Publication Data is on file with the publisher.

Source of Production: PrintPlus Limited, Shenzhen, Guangdong Province, China
Date of Production: June 2020
Run Number: 5017155

Printed and bound in China.
PP 10 9 8 7 6 5 4 3 2 1

SIDE A

1. Hit the Lights
2. The Four Horsemen
3. Motorbreath
4. Jump in the Fire
5. (Anesthesia) Pulling Teeth
6. Whiplash